A BOTTLE
AND OTHER POEMS

For Anthony Thwaite

Alan Brownjohn

A BOTTLE
AND OTHER POEMS

ENITHARMON PRESS

First published in 2015
by Enitharmon Press
10 Bury Place
London WC1A 2JL

www.enitharmon.co.uk

Distributed in the UK by
Central Books
99 Wallis Road
London E9 5LN

Distributed in the USA and Canada
by Independent Publishers Group
814 North Franklin Street
Chicago, IL 60610
USA
www.ipgbooks.com

ISBN: 978-1-910392-12-6

Enitharmon Press gratefully acknowledges the financial support of
Arts Council England, through Grants for the Arts.

Individuals contribute to sustain the Press through the
Enitharmon Friends Scheme. We are deeply grateful to all Friends,
particularly our Patrons: Colin Beer, Sean O'Connor and those
who wished to remain anonymous.

British Library Cataloguing-in-Publication Data.
A catalogue record for this book is available
from the British Library.

Designed in Albertina by Libanus Press
and printed in England by
Short Run Press

CONTENTS

A BOTTLE

On the beach in sudden sunshine, her turn:
Write down, she said, *the first
word you think of, we'll launch it
in the bottle.* And what they sent out
was *irretrievable.* Meanwhile, a wave
had carried their footwear away, which they
had left while paddling. Out to sea,
round the Point, past the Basalt Caves,
the tide carried all four examples and
the bottle with them. That lasted much longer
than the footwear, which the sea soon
bedraggled. Pretty well screwed up, so to speak,
the bottle stayed in one piece and was watertight,
it was one of several environmental flaws
deplored by persons on the deck of a boat
circling round an offshore windfarm;
the fisherman guide, running trips to see the seals on
a famous sandbank would have seen it too,
and maintained his silence. It floated on
past a hinterland where first there appeared
a bright and perilous resort from which
a rail link went out passing many fields
of oilseed rape, and horses freed
of their blankets for summer until, with long
moss-greened commuter platforms, a city
kicked in with capital's anonymous
glass megaliths. In one of those, an icon
guaranteed the manufacture of many
billions of similar bottles never to have
a mission like this one's . . . For weeks and weeks
it didn't make the shore, unlike the bodies
of two of the locally drowned and one
of the murdered . . . But at last a current

coaxed it into a lagoon where it finally
ended just inland on the purple verge
of a saltmarsh.

        His writing had been large,
with a felt-tip pen, in black, on good notepad paper,
and although the sun had faded it, the word
was still clear, *irretrievable*, when an inquisitive hand
unscrewed the cap – not easy – and fingered it out.
To be standing there in a marsh in the onset
of even a small contradiction dis-
composed him: he had retrieved both
the bottle and the old assumption that led
him to think it must be a letter inside it.
The bottle, now an irrelevant messenger,
he dismissed at once, but what you might call
the 'message' he kept. Against the odds, it raised
his confidence, if at moments he was disposed
to shiver and wonder whether he should just
let it go. But he did not do that, it was still
in his pocket on the day the two lovers
failed again to sense the treachery
of the tide and he, having read that one
extempore word, was at last tracked down
to 'this beautiful lonely stretch of the Oyster Coast.'

MUSICIAN
(for Jim Burns)

We knew he was coming down the hill from the sound
Of the Salon Orchestra or the Savoy Orpheans
Wound up to play for three minutes, then
Turned over for a second screeched melody,
The needle changed from a tiny box of the same.

We saw the sadness of the trolley pushed on
To its next port of earshot, and braked again with a wad
Of cardboard under the wheels, and new doors opening
Along the road for more of us to come out
With pennies begged from our mothers.

They didn't want to encourage this ancient man
In the bowler hat and ageless dark grey coat,
And his old horn gramophone with the bag of sweets
On the lower shelf, which is why we asked for pennies.
The other queer thing was, he never spoke.

ONE OF MYSELF

The lights arrive with a blink in a street of snow,
Outlining the shapes of trees. A figure slow
-ly approaches step by small step to where I take
Photographs balancing on the ice.
                                    Do I make
Sense to this Chinese stranger when I ask
Him for one of myself? It's a trivial task
So he agrees, and tries to understand,
With his gloves removed, exactly how to hand
-le my tiny Kodak before his fingers freeze.
Do I care if he fails?
                        No, because his expertise
Was complimented, like mine in other places
When asked to snap a variety of faces
For their families, friends, or posterity, or sometimes only
Themselves, to gaze at if they were lonely
On a snowy night.
                    Alone this summer, I
Scan a younger self and praise his accuracy.

AS NO ART IS

The weekend's on us, and no means of soothing it
or kissing it away. The flat façades
of mansion blocks curve towards silence. The sun
gets everywhere in this canyon, but property
holds its desperations in: the same flying ant
is all that moves along the same trouser folds.

I go to the park for late afternoon to arrive
among the memorials in their set-back space,
their immortality in the last century,
their short life-spans. What settles on this time
is not a haze or mist, but a half-visible
moderation of the light among the trees;

in which appear the hour-long married with
their picture-takers, from the distance down
the long paths hurrying, where sunlight falls
on patches between fallen leaves spread flat
by sudden July showers. Two by two they come,
the new from the known-to-each-other easily told

by the lonely watching eye; and stiffly stand
under their chosen heads of coiffured stone,
to smile once more – once more – and be caught,
in a flash or without one, at the most real,
the most complete, time of their day or night.
– Then it's all done with, and their hands are free.

I told her once, *Regard the eternal ocean*
as a comfort in your unremitting life.
It was only one day in six in our routines
we could sit there and watch it, I myself
walked from the Commissioners for Oaths, and she
from the Public Library. We sat in
a clifftop shelter at lunchtime, though only out
of season, you could not rely
on it being free in many other months.
We would kiss there, and it warmed us in the cold;
She would agree, I think ... But there were days
I had too much to undertake, oh just too much
– and I couldn't let her know, there was
no way of telling her at all, or her
telling me. Therefore it sometimes came
to waiting, waiting – please consider this –
for another seven days. And when you've done
three spells of seven-day waiting you start to wonder.
The days become their own independent country.
We didn't know if nothing, or everything,
was taking root without us, and filling
other people's memories of our special shelter
in the October or November of that year,
and perhaps even December, I can't be sure.
I remember, though, that we went in any weather,
and watched the leaves changing from the top
of the cliffs on the trees downhill from our haven
above the autumn sea; and I do recall
that before the end it refused us any comfort.

ARE ETCETERAS NO THINGS?
(Henry IV, Pt. 2)

Yes, usually. Except – some of the Things you don't remember in detail, but need to allow for, may include Very Important Things you unconsciously preferred to leave out.

They may have trailed away from your memory like the Smoke along the landscape, disappeared from where the Lovers on the hillside might have seen it when they raised themselves from the grass. They wanted to see the Train, but by then even the smoke from its engine had gone, resigning itself to the Air over the fields.

Or like protesting faces admitted to an imperial courtyard as a deputation, only to have the Great Door closed on them so they become as they turn away like any other faces in the crowd of Etceteras passing randomly in the street.

Or think of a list of somebody's Lovers, too long to recite even in sworn confidence to a patient friend. Ending with people too far-off to be remembered apart from the quaintness of the clothing they removed. But certainly once, yes, Very Important.

And how, out of that, at the tail-end of a year, in its last Etcetera days, there could return to somebody a blurred figure walking towards them who, in the last ten yards, is clearly focused again. Who places a hand on an arm and draws close saying , 'It Was Meant To Be Like This.'

We were registered as a form, and for the first day
Left unsupervised alone in a distant room
With empty desks to organise our own war.
Using books and inkwells was the easy way
Of creating bombardments – conkers and apple-cores came
In useful also, and in the master's drawer
There were sheets of exercise-paper which would acquire,
When neatly folded, the speed of darts to fly
Sharply across to send warnings of attack.
All the heads on the side of the classroom under fire
Dipped for cover under desk-lids when this weaponry
Rained down on them – to be picked up and fired back –
Though I don't recall any sort of hurt or harm
Resulting from this conflict, which was allowed
To go on uninterrupted, lasting throughout
Our entire first day of secondary term.
I remember each voice calling, on either side,
Its urgent orders, in a shrill, treble shout:
'Fire!' or 'Take shelter – Get down, everyone!'
I can still see Tim Hodgkiss lowering his face
Below his wooden shield, with no blood on it,
And there behind him – with all his limbs – Rex Dunn
Shooting darts and missiles from his usual place
In the back row out of sight, and the First Form wit,
Clive Pardew, in one piece, not in the sack thrown
Down elsewhere for collecting him. The real war
Was still young enough to have ended, like our own,
Except it didn't. – 'Fire!'? – 'Get down, everyone!'?
I can't hear treble voices any more
– They've changed, into an uncalled-for baritone.

A TABLE

And could there actually have been
a genuine craftsman cutting round
a line drawn on a sheet of glass
to cut this surface where I sit
in meditation waiting for
our dinner to be served on it?
This smooth transparent table top?
I can see my companions' knees,
including one of hers who has
to cross her legs to stop herself
falling forward onto her plate
in one of her perennial faints –
wisely she eats just special foods . . .
And there are two cold pairs of legs
owned by two married pillars of
an investment bank, who will not save
a factory I know between
a town I know as well, and its
dilapidated railhead, three
kilometres out across the plain. Three
hundred worked there last spring,
behind the windows now left dark
and shattered, and I knew well
some former workers, and their wives.
For several minutes I have seen
where the hands are going,
from etiquette, courtesy or nerves,
or just small things to do, while all
our deathly colloquy goes on,
first names exchanged as if
we had no others and were friends.
But now at last the point is reached:
the food is here, and down below

becomes a closed-off space of crumbs
and shoes and feet inside them
fidgeting. An obvious daring deed
occurs to me: I mean the dive
I sometimes did when very small,
under the surface, to be far
away from talk like this
– and want to do to-night.
(Except, I might be missed, or seen
embarrassingly between
servings, through the top of this
table I wish I was not at.)
I wish I had the strength.

THE WAY DOWN

There was no upward struggle required of me at the start.
I was the fourth generation of deference,
And grew into my father's clothes, inheritor
Of every grade of courtesy, always attending
With smiles and nods and obedient retreatings.
One day the golden lid closed on my hand
And my enemies heard the howling.

It was the winter of the triple dip.
I set up selling bling from unlicensed stalls
Where my line of talk worked till my illicit goods
Dropped out of fashion. I did keep a cheap guitar,
But was moved on from all likely underpasses,
And went from town to town unbuckling backpacks
Or lifting handbags from under tea-room chairs.

The indignity drove me mad, after all I'd been
A serving man proud in heart and mind, up for anything
The role required. Now it comes down to a wall
To sleep or lean against, and the dripping dregs
Of somebody else's can. They think a devil
Has taken me, but the truth is I've only arrived
In the first generation of despair.

AN AFFIRMATION

My front door slams behind me as I leave,
And for a moment I could quite believe

Someone real did it to be rid of me.
But God no! – come on – a draught took the liberty

Of ending this particular scene, a space
Where I hadn't closed a window caused the place,

Which I was leaving for around an hour,
To take on momently a curious power

To exclude me as unwelcome. But I can come back,
There is nothing to prevent me, and I don't lack

A key to get in with, thank you, my hand can feel
It there in its usual pocket and it's real.

I might have understood such a curt goodbye
For an absence of months or weeks, though I do try,

For spells like that, to tidy it and ensure
That when I walk in again I feel secure

Despite my shivering at the too-patient look
Of rooms long not eaten or slept in, and the book

Still unopened on a chair. And some new dust might
Have laid a tangible surface on the bright

Planks of the swept and polished floors,
And slowed the action of my ancient doors,

Requiring me to be firm about my claim
To be living there, even if it looks just the same

As when I left . . . Still, things being what they are,
Even though I don't intend to be going far

I shall take the hint, and as I walk away
Affirm hereby that I *shall* be back. Today.

LE TOMBEAU DE PORTER
i.m. PNFP
with love and gratitude

TRANSFORMATION

When I see Nadia's Nail Paradise,
Two minutes from Oxford Circus, I wonder
Could she transform me for whatever lies
Ahead, in my first date with the girl
From the Health Club reception at half-past five?
Would it be Nadia herself, or just Teresa
Providing her with my elegant surprise?

Would I go for Acrylic Infill or Full Set Gel,
To take this city in delicate strong hands
And bend it with easy arrogance to my will?
In the window opposite on the Northern Line
I am a changed man, Nadia worked a spell
To bring out the real self I always wanted:
The poised individual who cannot fail.

In this coffee bar waits a girl who probably went
For Nadia's Special Evening Make-up,
Only Ninety Pounds. I feel spent
Already when she mentions 'a friend',
His remarkable physique, the time she spent
In bed with him in the last two days alone.
How can she dare to be so eloquent?

I stare at another window now, and see
The brand-new lover I dreamt of reflected
In a loveliness I shall never be
Capable of attaining. Well, I tried,
But she has labelled me as 'enemy'.
My small dull fingers have turned to lead.
Nadia's flyer says, *Please recycle me.*

At eight you could not have foreseen
The fate of Jason, the silent boy
Never seen to use a calculator
Who would graduate from two Cambridges
By nineteen, and inherit the quietest room
In the Silicon Valley of his dreams,
Sectioned into it for his own
Protection from what his psychic fantasies
Instructed him to do when he saw them on the screen,
No more than you would have believed
Arabella, the winner of the Governors' Prize
For modelling, would be prised
From the different clay where the handsomest
Face from her Book would bring her
Having taken her out to the first
And last Margarita she ever attempted,
Or realise all that lay ahead
For Melanie was the boating lake
In the respectable suburb where she paddled
To the centre and held down her lover's child
Beyond any tremor of the water's surface,
Or if guessing any of these you might
Have forwarded faster than you did
To the day when you finished
The school run, and turned at the same door
To notice the mongrel abandoned after Christmas
Run barking at the one child who ever
Walked to school, and require to be
Restrained at the moment when
The reporter from Home Counties CTV
Just happened to be passing with
Camera and microphone and took
An interview for an early evening slot
On the difference a Big Society has made
To the ordinary dutiful citizen.

I ignored the bland cantatas enlisted
for the commercials, read on past the euphemistic
titles on the packaging, until I reached
the truth in the small print with the plain word *Death*.
I could not refuse it,
though I had the option of regarding it
as either inescapably important, or as trivial
just because there was no other way.
It was not user-friendly in that
I could not know when it would take effect,
although some ingredients went to the eyes,
the knees and the arteries (in my case at least)
and apprised me of what I could look forward to.
The advice from the leaflet inside
was certainly comprehensive. Fearing the contents
would make no difference, to enjoy
the prospect of them would disconcert your friends,
and bewailing it and its accomplice product, Time,
would just bore them if you did it too frequently.
To pass it on to others, most of all if their own
situations suggested they could do with it,
was profoundly wrong and illegal in all
acceptable cultures. Who first produced it
was immaterial, whether the idea came
from evolution, or was from the start
designed as the conclusion by a Creator who
(as some misguided persons will maintain)
required we believe in a Special Offer
that cancelled its effects with a proper application.
There was something curious about it being
always available from the start without anybody
being conscious of its power until the arrival
of sentient beings like ourselves.

I didn't enjoy knowing that a product forced
so widely on everyone right from the beginning
never varies in its final results.
Its side-effects, unlike those
of some remedies prescribed to counter it,
could give wonderful enrichment or consolation
and even left me feeling I wasn't bound
to take this product seriously after all:
huge edifices, resonant sounds, elaborate
formulations of brain and tongue would be
the experience of lucky ingestors of this thing.
On the other hand I suppose I am prepared
to accept it, particularly as
the salesman forcing it into my hands
collapsed on the doorstep peacefully, itself
a recommendation. I should nevertheless
like a chance to consider in detail exactly
what it might entail for a little longer.

Is there in the sudden adjustment of the deep freeze
To allow the last restless birds in the square to speak
Inaudible arpeggios of how indestructible it will be
When it arrives tomorrow, with an unswerving
Certainty that it has to happen?
The world is so finely modified Longinus
Shudders and rises on two front paws and yawns.
Is he redeemed or damned by what he cannot do
With the codex of his real time, and what
It challenges me to accept, as contrite as
A late answer to a letter or the frisson of
A ticket to Strelsau for tomorrow night?
It's not his talent to advise me,
I shall never know if he could, and besides
In cat-years at twelve he is older and wiser than me,
And immaculate in discretion.

SIGMUND FREUD AT SWISS COTTAGE

His forward leaning is a listening mode
no coalition could ever convince with. Between Little Hans
and the Wolf-Man he must have perfected this.

His hands rest on his hips as if all gesture
was insufficient, a form of attention so drastic
you'd have to open to it all your inner fabric.

One has to remember this is Vienna, not Paris,
given neither to hysteria nor hypnosis.
The snow makes its own submissions here,

and rests its empathy on his head and shoulders.
December enhances his middle-distance stare
and the summer cat who slept under him on his plinth,

out of reach of that fixed, eternal gaze,
was given his name and became iconic;
by the time its finale arrived with a dissonance

of brakes outside the backpackers' hostel,
it had merited a commemorative event.
There are some mysteries destined to endure.

What should a moggy named after him be thought
to have said for the local German saint to listen to
with all the stone furrows on his earnest brow?

*   *   *

IN REYKJAVÍK
Homage to Porter (and Auden)

Peter, I don't think – unless I've misremembered –
That you made it to this place, where the City Library
    Backs onto the harbour, and an inscrutable lift
Delivers a fifth floor 'Work and Study Centre'
    Well away from the banks of books that tempted you
Too much to compose in a well-stocked library.
    Even here, though, you might have found
The videnda too plausible for serious work:
    The low near hills look as friendly and unvolcanic
As any could be, but look up beyond them,
    And there's something ice-capped and glacier-like . . .
Some distances are better left alone,
    And here the turbulent hinterland or interior
Produces not broad-hatted bandits rendering all
    Railways unviable as soon as they went private,
But simply no solid ground for tracks, with three hundred
    Minor earthquakes a month around its rim.
Better my harbour foreground, where clean-painted vessels
    Cluster round a grey hulk of Fishery Protection,
Small apparently, but compare the size of the one man
    Walking down there beside the waters, strayed
Like a solemn ant from the follies of the rest.
    Would you have enjoyed the thought of a library
Where there are only single-chair tables facing
    In the same direction, no distracting faces,
No girls who must be quite as intelligent
    As they are beautiful, their glasses prove it,
To waste your time with gazing and speculation?
    – I think you *would* like it. Down below
Is an ample Foreign Section, meaning our language.
    Auden has made it there, but would you be found
In a separate Australian enclave? I hope in both.

Are you done into Icelandic? Wystan was,
For all their reservations about his trip,
   And was received with honour on his return.
Just how very long could and did the horses
   Bear that easily distracted traveller?
What did he really make of the lack of landscapes
   To play nostalgia with, so trolls and ogres
Became the order of the trip?
                       Now *I'm* distracted:
   Does any library offer finer seagulls?
Even to wonder that is to be drawn away
   By something other than fellow-students' faces,
And I think it might take a second and later visits
   To this fifth-floor room above the shining harbour
For the serious thinking to begin. Rather less brightness
   On the August waters, and more resolve, might provide
For that if I am lucky, rain and greyness
   Result in sonnets or pantoums, things deserving
Something more than just the patient, encouraging smile
   You should have been here to provide.

Will further words come with the wine
I sink alone at half-past nine,
The local grape help with all these
Grammatical necessities?
I doubt it.
        Yet this bottle gleams
With various self-improvement schemes,
And so once more I fill my glass
Quite unaware that pure disas-
ter lurks twelve hours from now . . .
                    Drink sends
Me forward hopefully, and lends
A sense of satisfaction to
The brisk revisions I pursue
For want of more romantic ways
Of seeing out these foreign days.
Muttering verbs under one's breath
May not disperse the fear of death
But now the air-conditioning hums,
And slowly the subjunctive comes!

THE SHIP OF ENDURANCE

Some opt for the Terrace, the sunshine, the breeze,
And divide between tourists – letting in the draught
By taking their time to saunter through the glass doors –
And locals, who go out quickly. The tourists ignore altogether
The people preferring to sit at the tables inside,
And deliver the café a hurricane – single
Pages from broadsheet papers – notes on lectures – credit
        slips
With precious landline numbers that took months
To extract from their owners – inspirations
That just had to be written down – there they go,
Chasing over the just-swept floor, people's whole days
Lost in fury and despair . . . Therefore I thank
The tall mindful local woman who when
She went out herself only opened the Terrace door
At the most acute angle enabling her to escape
– And before that had gathered up all my flying poems
In her hand to return them to me.
                       I dream up awards
For the – strictly speaking unrequired – courtesies
That make up the threads which hold the Ship of Endurance
Together. But all I can do for the moment
Is thank you, sincerely, Karin Johannesdottir,
Even though your business card speaks about 'IT'.

                       Akureyri, 2012

On the door, in their language, I think it says
We open at noon. We close at midnight.
We thank you for coming to see us.

It seems rather wrong for a pharmacist's,
But I am, after all, in a foreign country:
You have to understand the local rules.

The real chemist's shop turns out in the end to be
On the floor above, up some unseen stairs behind
(I've looked it up) the Grand Ice Cream Pavilion.

In this store, the man in front of me in the queue,
In years-long-worn-out clothes, as if he's on
Some endless ruined holiday, spends a long time

Buying all that he can afford, a tiny box
Of apparent vitamins for STRESS (I've looked
That up in the dictionary also, later on),

While his friend, even shabbier and half his size,
Has the look of suffering an even longer
Vacation from health, security and respect.

I am there to buy only what is recommended
By the pharmacist's assistant, obviously,
Our Own Fine Cream, You Can Only Buy It Here

– To protect my skin against the stressful sun . . .
I walk out into the unseasonal morning glare
From the lightly-scented shade of their premises,

And the two men lurch ahead of me. I muse
On despair, its abysses, its hoped-for remedies . . .
And wonder if these two, at their age, from long habit

And in subsumed surrender, have become the only
Remedy for each other.
                              Now a girl comes out
Of the door I had believed was the pharmacist's,

With a board: SAMPLE OUR ICE CREAM DELIGHTS.

WHAT THE MUSIC'S FOR

What do you think the music's for?

Don't know. Must it be for anything?

The music's for drowning the other music. And what
Do you think the drilling's for?

You mean the drilling always going on
Behind whatever you're doing, wherever you are?
Always stopping and starting? These days everywhere
Drowning your chances of being heard, or hearing?
Don't know either.

The drilling is part of our culture, like the music.
It's for making and building more of the things we believe in.

What kind of things do you mean? And what do I believe in?

Things made for hands, and the fingers on hands, and for legs,
And the families that provide them. Things like guns for hands
And like buttons for fingers to press, and drones to send out
To find and destroy our culture's enemies.
You must believe in all those.

And the legs?

The legs are for forming lines and for drilling and marching
To the music, which has changed to a stronger rhythm.
We believe in the music, it's all about moving on
From anything kind and familiar, love for example –

But love –

Kindly let me finish, I didn't interrupt
When you were asking questions. Love is finished,
Love is not for rocks and sand.
                                See – there they go,
The hands, the fingers, the guns, the legs,
Across thousands of miles of sand and rock stained
With the honour of history while the drones
Drone honourably ever onwards above them
To the sound of the music.

And the families?

They have been told.

A poet whom I didn't much admire
Said before he died (in fact some years before,
At ninety), 'Time chases past ever faster, one's daily dose
Of the same old medication – down it goes
About five minutes after the last. But then things
Many decades ago feel closer than this morning.'
– Then, having to shave, I remembered the seconds hand
Chasing round the classroom clock, last lesson, and
Rosemary's whisper: 'Do you know *this* one?' – and moving
Her forefinger nail round and round contriving
A slow tickling circle on my extended palm.
Unbearable, but pleasant. Yes, concerning time
And memory he was right: That was five to four
The day the Japanese entered Singapore.

In a side-street shuttered first-floor room a Blonde,
Mature and Sympathetic, dropping off
In the middle of a slack winter afternoon
Has a dream;
                    of an ancient car she travelled in
When she was seventeen and pretty strong.
It would frequently break down, and she would take
The starting handle,
                    and turn and turn and turn
To fire the silent engine of that Alvis,
Later sold to me by a friend who had a friend
Who bought it from her father,
                                    who could rely
On his daughter's willingness and strength
As often as not. After about ten cranks
The thing would jerk and buzz to everyone's
Relief and satisfaction;
                                which her dream brings back:
The car, the rainy long days spent out
On the North Kent coast, that triangle of crime
Related to high scrapyards of caved-in cars,
The days of endless quarrelling from the start
Between her parents,
                        who were together then . . .
Someone once asked her if she'd enjoyed that job,
To which she answered *Yes*, and to *Why on earth* –?
– *I liked to feel it tremble in my hand.*

The thing that this moment
roared past the man who
stood up on the platform,
that blared its horn,
that brightened its lights,
that tilted its liqueur in
the exquisite direction
of the virgin princess just
today sent into exile

performed all that in his
imagination only, his paranoia being
of the superior kind.
To him it would never
have occurred that this train
on which he closed his eyes
for the dreams and dreads
to work, was the five to twelve
for all stations to Nothing,

serving fast foods only, all
table-seats snaked-and-laddered
especially for the bored,
each hooded face illumined
by a screen with no meaning,
the entire shooting star
powered on through the night
by the dullest envies he
could never have imagined . . .

And who was missing out,
the one standing alone
with false fears of disrespect

in the silence regaining itself?
Or the jealousies roaring on
at the speed of progress,
without any words at all
in the dark and the cold
for the cold, for the dark?

He believes he is awake, but no he isn't.
He is still in the dream, and admits that, saying aloud,
'I am dreaming this, and in a clammy sweat.
And what is the origin of "clammy"?'

Then someone is closing the door, he knows
It's his real bedroom door from the sound of it.
His former partner is coming across the floor
Towards the bed. She gets into it beside him.

'Where did you go to be so late?' he asks,
With a yawn that almost forces him back to sleep.
Without a word she clambers over him into
Her usual sleeping position for several years.

He is conscious, very conscious, of dreaming now
Because a second shape has entered the room
By the same means, and entered the bed on the side
Still vacant, asking, 'Who is that English woman?'

He is vulnerable enough to feel trapped by this.
'I have the assurance that I *can* wake up
When the dream has reached closure,' he thinks.
'But I haven't the least idea how to get it there.

'Through several layers of subconsciousness
I circle round in nightmare. The door has vanished
And yet, after months of sweating travel
I have reached it at last. I grip the handle,

'But my hand is clammy and slipping. Purchase on
The handle of anything has never proved
So hard . . . Except, I've done it. It turns. It opens.
I am there in the bed again. I hear the door.'

PROVISIONALITY

Will the sea grow tired on a warming earth,
or lash at the stanchions below
somewhile after we have all left?
In our Pierhead Doubles Saloon
the barperson serves pushing back
two strands of errant hair over
her ear, upending a careful
optic into a glass to slide over
to a wordless patron. She includes
a smile that begins but then stops,
and goes no farther.
                                   Out there
a white sail flaps and flattens
on blue-black waters, I hear
a ball in the Games Room batted
to and fro to and fro. The silent
man lifts his glass, and no one
speaks in the corner where three
sit in black and grieve, and remember.
A short figure on the beach
swims out quickly the final
few minutes of day, helped in
by the incoming tide. On frozen
feet through the shallows, he shivers up
to a wooden cabin and there
takes off wetsuit and flippers, he'll eat
with a chum when I spot him later,
in Mr Moon's restaurant in town,
his hair still damp from his triumph,
and be served by Miss MINA WEN LUO
as her name disc relates.
                                   We're at
a delicate point in all

our autumn experience, but doubt
if anyone else sees that.
Life darkens, as day does, I go back
to her 'Service Point', the words
in her Job Specification. She
says, 'The old city is the best part,'
the barperson, recommending Riga.
'Well, who wants to live or work on
the twenty-third floor any place
on earth?' I agree. And hang on,
even when she swivels and presses
four further measures, and tilts them
into two more glasses. Her half-smile
resumes and stops; I ask her,
'Are there Latvian friends you have here?'
'No I haven't . . . There aren't.' 'But some English?'
'Yes. Allison. Working part-time
as a nurse in – how do you call it? –
a hospice. We were talking once
when she was here, and suddenly
we became friends. [Alli helps them
to go by day, and others to come
by night, in her clifftop apartment.'
But that she just thinks, doesn't say.]
Downstairs the sea fulminates and
new moonlight is wanting
the breakers to stop and allow
a calm path of light to pass over
the multiplied wave. I ask,
'Will you go back to Riga?' 'I don't know,
not yet.'
          A bewildering ball,
our planet . . . Is anyone hoping

for anything soon? All this world
seems provisional and waiting.
An hysterical spray bursts up
at the end of the promenade walkway
'like' it has, they will say, for as long
as anyone can recall, going on
despite the warming, high tides
still trying from habit. The town
shines indifferent lights on
quiet walkers, and suicides
in the local next week.
                    Who else,
if I don't, will recall this
unchangeable afternoon?

Among the things I am mostly happy doing,
One needs a white page, another requires a white sheet.

The work on the white page demands ideas.
For the white sheet a suitable word might be dreams.

A great German poet once wrote that he counted beats
On the back of a beloved between white sheets.

One concluded that only genius could blend
The two distinct purposes in such a style,

Since mainly the two remain wholly separate,
And a difficult choice requires to be made:

Those in favour of the white page, please raise their hands . . .
Those in favour of the white sheets, please do the same . . .

Abstentions?

MOVEMENT

Ten minutes – or less – before we step down at one
of the 'London Terminals', ploughed land restarts
and the newest cow-parsley spreads by the side
of fields that held on through the April drought.

The immediate foreground is dashing on past
a stationary middle-distance while
a forest on the horizon, darkly capped
by clouds, races forward at the same speed.

It's comforting that the laws of perspective and motion
apply as I saw them, forty years back, in some lines
about love and apprehension. These fields we pass
are still, as before, to be considered the green

foundation of everything, sending out kind seeds
into city yards and squares. But some cooling towers
recur here for all their reputed demolition,
and as the suburbs begin mini-hangars appeal

for 'sellable parts'. Then arrive some further shots
at edgeland enterprise, and a wide terrain
of tracks where it has long been banned and burnt
appears to purge our consciousness of grass.

It insists that moving onwards must come first.
We are where it all ends, people holding hands
into this Terminal for consolation,
and we have to step down. It doesn't look like love.

Need history be kinder to apprehension?

TAKES
(*i.m. A.J.T.*)

1

You ran from place to place and mission
to mission. And smiled as you told me
that to do all this safely you needed
your lucky ribbons with their childhood name,
taken everywhere in your bag. If you lost those,
they were irreplaceable. Except, you did replace them,
painful though it felt. And went on running.

2

How could you know a meeting was complete?
That the most important questions wouldn't come
When the landscape was passing the train window?
What did you take from *our* meetings? I tried to give
the answers before your questions, spelt out so much . . .
Were we building something? I wanted
To be able to stand back and look at it.

3

You took time from work to ring. Diaries,
finding them in a chaos of obligations.
'Hi! – *I'm sorry I didn't get back to your call'*.
'Doesn't matter. You've done it now. So, then.
When are you free? I'm searching my diary, can
you hear that?' '*Yes . . . And I'll get mine out for you.*'
Beyond your words a wave of office laughter.

4

It became a custom on leaving. At
the foot of my ten steps I'd walk round you

making space for two antique courtesies:
first, yield you the inside of the pavement,
second, take the lighter from your hand
and try to work it, failing, for your one
apologetic drag of the whole night.

5

Under the franked postmarks with clear red dates,
your writing on the long cream envelopes.
I'd take out one – two – A4 pages . . . *perhaps a lovely*
excuse to meet? . . . so sorry for my tired state . . .
time to let our hair down soon . . . See you next week . . .
I will call to confirm . . . but one never knows.
Would you have guessed I was keeping everything?

6

Winter hardening, the latest long
Security straggle, sleet falling. Once inside,
I hoped you'd be taken in the queue behind me,
the next to be flashed and stored. But you got sent
to a different camera. There I stand
with only a grey blank behind me . . . That time, though,
you came back, smiling. We were let through, and safe.

7

Memory takes its altered pictures later,
improving and adding if you want it to.
Once, as a child, I believed you could just take image
on image, to keep; though you'd get too many
to live in the present. I have you walking round

before sitting down at the table. When you talked there,
all your recall came out like photographs.

8

We agreed to exchange some when you came back
from the mission to St Petersburg: books we hadn't read,
our long and shameful lists. *This Side of Paradise*
I gave you, and *The Line of Beauty* you took
the trouble to parcel up and send me.
I can't recall if you'd seen what I had read there,
by chance: words meaning this was Tchaikovsky's grave.

9

What I keep thinking is: I praised it as
'Your original storm-blue gown,'
just the thing for a vindictive, drenching summer.
It was while you lingered by the table
the final time, and I held you for just as long
as I thought you'd let me. – That clever reference
echoes too much. Ahead of an event.

10

One small-print instruction is *How
to Delete the Last Voicemail.* Just as easy
is *How to Delete all Voicemails.* But I look
for *How Not to Mistake the Second
Instruction for the First.* And I can't find that.
I can't remember when, from fear, on impulse,
I taped your only messages, just in case.

11

Months after those first times I can't believe
I'm driving home on a motorway, high on my list
of what makes life implausible. Is it only
minutes it takes for ashes to cool? For it
to be impossible ever to say, Go away,
get on with all of it, but please come back
after ever-shortening spells of our future time?

12

A few hours forgetting, then a wave
of guilt at forgetting. Try going back
to do this take once more. It wasn't right.
Walk back from the dark again. And smile again.
Be as you were, as we remember you.
Yourself. Yes, you're coming through. Now turn, walk –
Walk towards us. Yes. You've got it. Perfectly.

Randomly, sleet that night becoming snow,
Requests you merely met, but hugged demands
Rudderless, our slow craft surely
Sex can be relevant – *But the thing to learn*
Single departures. One by one, leaving
Somewhere the one green county your
Take care was all their advice, who never
Tell me again, Eurydice, what should I
Undertows and underworlds
Vanity Fair came high on a shaming list
Velvet feet took ten steps. His leap, an arc
'We understand your wishes but can't grant
X meaning *Extra Size*, not the Spot where
You were not there to praise the play. I thought
Z, z, *zed*, noun, twenty-sixth and last

In the middle of a batch of junk
one with her writing, these days
the postmark uninformative . . .
It might be precious. The smaller
kitchen knife opens it, and I'll keep
the envelope because it's part of her.

The contents are a jade green-
twice-folded half of a torn A4,
spelling out NO MORE WORDS.
Well at least I didn't this time have
to pay for the lack of a stamp. – *I'm sorry?*
– *Yes. I'll still keep the envelope.*

NEVERTHELESS

Like the machine the day had churned in dark circles,
But when at last I came back the whole contraption
Had stopped too soon, all its baggage had halted
In a stubborn wish to stay there and nowhere else.
I wouldn't know when this had happened,
Maybe some time in the first half-hour while I
Was abroad it had issued a rap, a shudder,
A shake, and a stillness. Its red warning
Stayed alight on the closed door. Its water
Wasn't going to break into any outlet,
Its porthole gave onto a darkness that refused
Any sound or movement, and I found myself
Looking out for comfort at a clear night sky.
It hadn't stopped.

THE LIGHTS
(*for Martina Evans*)

When the lift doors open, the radiographer
Sees thirty persons, many more than she would prefer,
Two of whom hold someone up. They all shuffle
Up the corridor towards her, and there's a scuffle
To get to Reception first and be proud to explain
That here is a famous Belfast player, in pain
From a floodlit collision half-an-hour ago,
And he can't stand on that leg. Will an X-ray show
If he's broken something?
                              Meanwhile in Shenzhei
A girl pulls down towards her a lamp with a high-
Energy bulb in it in an attempt to find
An ambivalent instrument left behind
By a grandparent's visitor. This might unseal
Certain family secrets, and as result reveal
What an upstairs drawer of junk which has long
Puzzled her really means. She could be wrong,
But it's worth the try – except, the bulb burns out,
So she's still in the dark for now.
                                    And who would doubt
That darks can be dangerous . . . But a bank of snow
Slides down from a Ford's 'bonnet' – even though
A 'hood' is what it's called in the USA –
And covers the headlights, no one can say
If they are on full, or dipped – or not on at all –
And two lovers walking the road, where they might not fall
As they might on an icy sidewalk, are therefore not seen
By a husband driver. There might have been
A skid if he had braked, and an accident,
Which the shifting of the snow serves to prevent.
Thus the lovers are allowed two escapes: their affair
Stays secret for one more week, and they get a rare
Postponement of death. This is their one
Short spell of luck in Portland, Oregon.

MARCH SNOW

It lies in strips on branches as if that were arranged
For somebody to paint them. It's sprayed on the backs
Of four chairs left leaning over a garden table
When a meal was stopped by the August rain.
I need to be out, so get most carefully
Down the eight steps to the pavement and press a catch
To spread against the wind a black dome lacking
One spoke which is broken, at least protecting
One half of me, on a late March afternoon.
The snow sweeps at my ankles from where the street
Has been collecting it in the cause of silence.
Above my head the ceaseless pattering
Goes on, not like rain, like the lightest fingers
Come back to drum on a window expecting
To be let in and understood despite it all.

THE OLD DELIGHT
(a toast to Martin Bax at 80)

Dear Martin, welcome to Octopolis,
A proud, if fearful, city but greatly worth
Living in, no question. The longer
I inhabit it myself the more I believe
I'll go on relishing all that you've always
Given me as writer, doctor, friend:
Wise judgements, deep encouragement, all kinds
Of medical wisdom – and, of course,
Nights out on tiles more slippery than before
But still, in your company, possible to tread
With the old delight. Here's to you for all of that!

BAR MIRROR

He had not recognised me or I him.
The place was crammed and rackety, and our eyes
Took each other in, and we didn't realise...
We stared, and we ruled each other out until
After several glassy seconds I found the will
And the nerve to speak. Well – it must be! – He knows my
name.

In the warmth that dropped on me after the ice-cold air,
I'd been looking for someone I knew, to launch a greeting
Eagerly after long decades of never meeting.
In a crowd of loud unknowns I would still have said
I might tell this man from the back of his schoolboy head,
And a sureness that the same face would still be there.

But whereas I'd kept down to a coating of grey
Hairs the strictures of time, he must have chosen
At some one point to cast his looks in this frozen
Fix of resolve: a magnate's air, or the stance
Of a judge or a general offering little chance
Of mercy or pardon to anyone in his way.

I couldn't say what experience – what *disease?* –
Might have changed his features to this curious form,
Maintaining them thus right up to the present time.
We had grown apart without ever dreaming that so
Much change would occur in us, and we'd just not know...
But there it was, in a shoal of differences.

And why hadn't we talked this through? We didn't doubt
It was too late to try now. We could only give
Cold acknowledgement to each other and try to live
In the next hours through the masks we had settled for.
So we stood and accepted that. We knew the score,
Like everyone else lost for things to talk about.

They start to say *autumnal* in the forecasts,
And on the Northern Line the shifting panels
Look bleached already. I think less about
The low-cost rivieras than the remedies
At the ends of small pale almanacs for afflictions
Acquired by the old, or suffered by loners
In the margins of respectable families
   – Ailments with names we don't use any more.

Each black-and-white ad in the narrow columns
Promised miracles on the same unlikely terms,
For the sender sitting in a bedroom corner
To seal an envelope bought that afternoon. . .
Could I even imagine one such to be my own,
With a man returning from a PO Box in Strood
And sending by return, as promised, the First Lesson
   In his course called *Why Not Join Me in the Coloured Pages?*

CHRISTMAS SCENARIO

'But sir, this is the time to celebrate.'
'No.' – I decline the Santa hat proffered me
By the waiter, and declare instead: 'Champagne
For the lady alone in the corner, if
She will accept it.' Thinking, 'She can't be driving.'

'You'll have to guide me for the final stretch',
I tell her. 'Oh, it's no problem now',
She assures me as we leave the motorway,
'Just follow the red signs.' In the twisting dark,
Through snow and trees and shadows I spin her wheel,

And, 'Do you live alone?' I ask her softly.
'If Strindberg hasn't been fed, I do to-night.'
A last bend, a brief avenue, we stop.
I switch off. A real owl hoots somewhere,
Or a taped owl plays in the nearby wood.

'Oh Strindy! Come on, then.' The Burmese cat
Wails on the mudguard of this replica,
And is fended off gently by her opening door.
We cut to the kitchen where the genius animal
Is made replete, then some ominous echoes

Follow our feet across a mosaic floor
To a room replete with incunabula
From God knows where, the only lamps are low.
As a heavy clock hand shifts towards the hour,
The champagne kicks in on my monthly statement.

Should I play the direct guy I should like to be?
I sit down opposite her uncertain

As to my or her motives. Turning she prises
A Malory from a convenient shelf, and smiles,
And opens it and takes out . . . [To be decided.]

THE ANSWER

I'll wait for you where I can tell you and no one hear.
Take these directions: turn half-left outside,
then follow the street which bisects the oppo-
site rightangle of the intersection. Pass
the Daylong Bar on your right
with its purple dome; you should recognise
the place – where the newly-slabbed pavement gets
uneven again alongside the site planned
for the new emergency hospital until last month.
Just think: it could have installed two hundred
stitches for mishaps on that stretch alone.
At this point the Centre has become
the suburbs, and the road awaits scheduled repairs.
They have chalk-marked – look – the opportunities
for revengeful potholes to assert their rights,
so walk warily past the Cross-themed railings of
the Third Church of Christ Consultant, and on
towards the unmistakeable Herm of
the Half-known Soldier with the eyes
that follow you to affirm that the Racial War
just ended was indeed the very last.
Oh, and here you find the final pharmacist
before the mountains, and on her favourite
verandah (note the spelling) Madame Slutski.
Look twice, because she's moving slightly,
being real and not her statue, waiting for
her quantitative lover to ride up
and ease her sorrows. At this point ask yourself
why verified history and the un-
illuminated present have to lock

pure evil and ignorance together
with stupidity in an endless chain.
– But keep going, keep going, keep
going. Stop! Here's a painted sign
saying WELCOME TO BETTER THINGS,
where a sharp incline starts suddenly,
and the road is a rocky slope. How far behind
the Last Upstairs Billiard Hall seems
on the edge of the forest, and its rumoured bears
seen once by Grandma from her scullery window,
come down to trample the fuchsias;
or the indefinable fanged and clammy things
that eye you from small bushes predicting the treeline.
Still, keep on, keep on, and prepare to cherish
the thought that you are carrying several
boxes of Safety Matches in case
you need to strike them and throw them
at wolves appearing from nowhere,
You truly have passed the very last
outpost of civ-il-i-sa-tion, here
are rocks only, no vegetation, and that
is not the ultimate summit, the next one is,
or perhaps the one beyond it, or the one
beyond that. When you are sure you see it, stand
silent below it, and shake the snow
from your sandals, identify
the twenty-four-seven shadow thrown
by the hut where I am waiting.
Enter, greet me, put your hat down,
and remember to refer to the circle of deckchairs

on the sunny lawn, where the gameplan
was originally decided; and now you
are sure no one can hear me, ask me the answer.
Oh, I'll give it you to save time: You
yourself are the only answer.